COLOR YOURSELF INSPIRED

THE CAT LOVER'S

Creative Soul

COLORING BOOK

Print ISBN 978-1-68322-106-7

Cover illustration: Yee Von Chan
Interior illustrations: Yee Von Chan, Felicity French, Pimlada Phruapadit, Erica Salcedo, Angelika Scudamore, Kat Uno

Published by Barbour Books, an imprint of Barbour Publishing, Inc., P.O. Box 719, Uhrichsville, OH 44683, www.barbourbooks.com

Our mission is to publish and distribute inspirational products offering exceptional value and biblical encouragement to the masses.

Member of the
Evangelical Christian
Publishers Association

Printed in the United States of America.

COLOR YOURSELF INSPIRED

THE CAT LOVER'S

Creative Soul
COLORING BOOK

BARBOUR BOOKS
An Imprint of Barbour Publishing, Inc.

Everything *that* moves serves to interest & amuse a cat.

François-Augustin de Paradis de Moncrif

Everything
God made
is
good.

1 Timothy 4:4

Trust
God's
Wisdom...
& keep *your*
claws in.

May the Lord give you wisdom & UNDERSTANDING.

1 Chronicles 22:12

But it is you...
one who has gone with me,
my close friend.

Psalm 55:13

The touch of a paw
brings great comfort
and joy
to the
heart.

FOR I will change their SORROW to joy, and will comfort them.

JEREMIAH 31:13

Our hearts
are richer
for having
known our

feline
friends.

I HAVE GIVEN YOU A

Wise and
Understanding
heart.

1 KINGS 3:12

Cats

minister to our souls
through soft fur and
rumbling purrs.

Know in all your **HEARTS** and in all your **SOULS** that not one of all the good promises the Lord **YOUR GOD** made to you has been broken.

JOSHUA 23:14

Father God,

help me to care for my
cat wisely and well.

The Lord will take care of me.

PSALM 27:10

Cats have a curious effect on people.

ARTHUR PONSONBY

If there is anything good and worth giving thanks for, think about these things.

PHILIPPIANS 4:8

HE LETS ME REST
in fields of green grass.

HE LEADS ME BESIDE
the quiet waters.

PSALM 23:2

*Who would believe such pleasure
from a wee ball o' fur?*

Irish Saying

Being with You is to be full of joy.

Psalm 16:11

I love cats because I love my home,
and after a while they become its invisible soul.

Jean Cocteau

God makes a home for those who are alone.

Psalm 68:6

Keep on
GIVING
Your loving-kindness
to those who know You.

PSALM 36:10

BEFORE

a cat will condescend

TO TREAT YOU AS A TRUSTED FRIEND,

Some little token of esteem

IS NEEDED, LIKE A *DISH* OF

CREAM.

T. S. Eliot

CREAM

If having a soul means being able to feel *LOVE* and *LOYALTY* and *GRATITUDE,* then animals are better off than a lot of humans.

JAMES HERRIOT